A CHILD'S HISTORY OF HAWAII

Written and Illustrated by Hawaii's Children

To Edward Rutledge McGrath
and the children of Hawaii

A CHILD'S HISTORY OF HAWAII

Written and Illustrated by Hawaii's Children

ORIGINATED AND DIRECTED BY
EDWARD J. McGRATH JR.

EDITED BY
BOB KRAUSS

 An Island Heritage Book

Produced in Association with The State Foundation On
Culture & The Arts and The Hawaii State Library System

Edward J. McGrath
Project Director

Karen L. McGrath
Assistant to the Director

Kenneth M. Brewer
Assistant to the Director

Robert B. Goodman
Editor in Chief

Robert A. Spicer
Executive Editor

Carol A. Jenkins
Assistant Managing Editor

Robert F. Badham
Art Editor

George F. Fargo
Educational Editor

Terry Barrow
History Editor

Robert Krauss
Text Editor

Nella Hoffman
Art Director

Judy Albro
Trudi F. Fukamizu
Miriam T. Nakasone
Assistant Editors

Produced and published by Island Heritage Limited
Norfolk Island, Australia

For the Island Heritage distributor in your area,
please write or phone:

Island Heritage Limited (USA)
Editorial Offices
1020 Auahi St. Bldg. 3
Honolulu, Hawaii 96814
Phone: (808) 531-5091
Cable: HAWAIIBOOK

Engraving, printing, and binding by
Leefung-Asco Printers Ltd. Hong Kong

A Note to the Reader

In the words and pictures of Hawaii's children, this unique book is a living history of our islands. To achieve it, we asked our children to paint or write about their Hawaii; what they understood about how Hawaii came to be.

The children's response was overwhelming, a torrent of more than six thousand images and stories drawn with enthusiasm and love by children ranging in age from kindergarten to the eighth grade.

What they wrote about and painted they did with the total involvement that is so joyously part of childhood. There was real magic in the telling of their tales, a reaching out to touch other times and other generations.

A young boy became the volcano he wrote about. A young girl, writing about her grandparents, relived their hardships as they strove to build a family and a place for themselves in an alien land.

Boys became for a moment Kamehameha the Great. Girls became Queen Liliuokalani. One by one the special qualities that make Hawaii what it is were entered and explored by our children and made their own.

Out of their explorations, their insights and wholehearted involvement has come a tender story in book form. In this storybook, our children have given us, their parents, mentors and peers, an insight into the islands we live on that is filled with understanding, freshness and love.

A *Child's History of Hawaii* is a gift to us all.

The Editors of Island Heritage

THE ARTISTS AND WRITERS

Anthony Aila Jr.
Douglas Andersen
Aaron M. Anderson
Brian Arakawa
Sherry Artzt
Danet Ashley
Eric Au
Jeffrey Au
Russell Au
John Belles Jr.
Gib Bintliff
Aida Bitonio
Scott Brainard
Errol Burgos
Darlyn Camit
Darren Casaquit
Elisabeth Case
Beverly Casicas
Jane Cazimero
Andrea Chang
Gareth Chang
Darlene Ching
Melvin Ching
Valkyrie Chong
Cyrus Chun
Elizabeth Chun
Janice P. Chun
Sharon Chun
Alvin Chung
Shelly Chung
Michelle Clayton
Diane Clark
Susan Clegg
Stephen Clubb
Mercy Cole
B.B. Conger
Erin Connors
Janet Correa
Sarah Craven
Kim Crawford

Brian Scott Cua
Deborah Dagley
Sandra Dagley
Mary Davis
Lynnette De Lima
Sharon Delapina
Shelby Denman
Laura Denny
Robert L. Dodge Jr.
Reinhard Domen
Debra Downey
Roslynn Dunavay
Joanna Endo
Jan Enos
Susan Espiritu
Rosemary Estrella
Angel Fajardo Jr.
Elisa Floyd
Lisa Fowler
Jan Fugita
Faith M. Fujimoto
Ryan Fukuki
Ann Furukawa
Antonino Ganiron III
Monica Genadio
Cinda Lee Giarraputo
John Gibson
Rupert Gomes
David Andrew Goodman

Maile Lisa Goodman
Sterrett Grune
Billy Gursahani
Maile Guy
Dean Haggen
Colleen Hall
Lani Hanabusa
Billy Hannum
Karen Hashimoto
Len Hassler
Sandra Hatakenaka
David Hayes
Teryn Hee
Martin Heirakuji
Chris Hernandez
Judy L. Hess
Mark Hitchcock
Alton Ho
Heidi Ho
Kenton Ho
Lynn Marie Ho
Randy Holt
Eugene Echinose
Theresa Ichiriu

Susan Ignacio
Leonardo Inso
Tracy Ishikawa
Larry Jacinto
John Jenkins
Greg Johnson
Ivy Joseph
Nelson Julian
Morgan W. Justice Jr.
Albert Kaahaaina
Alan Kadota
Nathan Kadota
Dora Kahahane
Evelyn Kailikea
Kevin Kaito
Fay Kalanui
Lori Dianne Kam
Jason Kamakawiwoole
Gayleen Kamoku
Calvin Kaneshiro
Julie Kaohi
Warland Kealoha
Valerie K. Kealohi
Mary Colleen Kelley
Lee Kennedy
Kevin Kimata
Merlyn Kiyota
Ashlyn Klug
Fujiko Kobashigawa
Kim Kobashigawa

Walter Kobayashi
Allyn Kozai
Paul Krogh
Kordell Kubo
Kenneth Kwan
Douglas Lagua
Chris Lattig
Jonn Lau
Brandon Lee
Jeff Lee
Karen Y.C. Lee
Helen Leedy
Caroline Leong
Lance Leong
Marvalene Lindsey
Beryl Loo
Catherine Loo
Lionel Lopez
Patricia Luebbe
Andrew Lum
Joseph Lum
Melissa Lum
Naomi Lyum
Lee Mahiai
Marilyn Mangasar
Marc Matsubara
Earldeen Medeiros
Elaine Miller
Kelly Min
Marsha Miyata
Zenaida Molina
Gail Morikawa
Alison Moritsugu
Toby Morris
David Moss
Anne Mukaigawa

Debbie Nash
Dale Nees
Nathan Ng
Lani Nicholson
Derek Nirei
Mark Nishiyama
Russell Nonaka
Susan Nozaki
Sue Nozoe
Steven Ohata
Ronald Okabe
Jesse Okimoto
Donna Onaga
David Onasch
Monte Opperman
Georgette Ortiz
Arlene Oshiro
Kenneth Oshiro
Sela Oshiro
Alan Oshita

George Paris
Suzi Park
Naomi Patterson
Joann Perreira
Beth Peters
Paul Pilago
James Pililaau
Keith Pine
Elizabeth Plazzie
Edward Poe
Gwen Poe
June Rita
Harriet Roeder
Ross Rytting
Chiaki Sagami
D. Sakamoto
Dawn Sakamoto
Melvin Satterlee
Kirsten Savage
Gil Shaeffer
Cindy Scharsch
John Schmidt
Juanita Schmidt
Carolyn Schnack
Marjorie Schnack
Christian Schneider
Donald Schuab
Gunner Schull
Suzanne Schwab
Carolyn F. Scott
Petra Sherwood
Scott Simmons
Michael Simonds
Hannah Somerville

Kaleo Souza
Nathan Spencer
Julie Steckling
Ricky Sukita
Glen Sulliban
Paddy Sullivan
Brian Sweber
Jody Sylva
Noreen Tabuno
Marla Ann Takahama
David Takayesu
Diane Tamura
Sarah Tanner
Kenneth Terukina
Mat Thompson
Karen Tom
Terry-john Tomiyama
April Tong
Valrie Uehara
Evan Uyechi
Marvaly Ventura
Susan Vierra
Perfecta Domingo Villanueva
Scott Walker
Sherri Watase
Karen Watt
Mike Watts
Karen Weatherspoon
Jennifer White
Wesley Wilhelm
Carolyn Won
Francis A. Wong Jr.
Gary Wong
Lenbert Wong
Dawn Wright
Dwight Yamashita
Carla Yee
Keith Yonamine
Sandra Young
Darren Zimmerman

THE SPURTING VOLCANO

In the middle of the Pacific Ocean there was nothing. Hawaiian people were not born yet. If we were born, what would we stand on?

It just had the big blue and white ocean.

An old Hawaiian legend says one of the gods named Maui fished up the islands dripping wet from the ocean floor. But scientists say that the islands were made in a different way. When the time came, when dinosaurs lived on earth, a great crack began to open on the floor of the ocean three miles deep. It was a volcano.

Out of this crack, red and yellow fire rocks came. It was called lava, a hot liquid so hot it can melt anything. Lava was coming out so fast you wouldn't believe. When the lava touched the water it cooled up. The lava, piled up from the constant eruptions, shaped into mountain forms. This took thousands and millions of years. The constant eruptions caused the peaks of the volcanoes to rise. Above the ocean there was smoke because a volcano that erupts brings forth masses of gasses, dust and cinders.

Some of the mountains climbed into the sunshine and air. Years went by and still the volcanos kept erupting. The tops smoked and spouted. Lava streamed down the slopes and into the water. Giant clouds of steam shot into the air. The sea rose and went down. The volcanoes kept erupting.

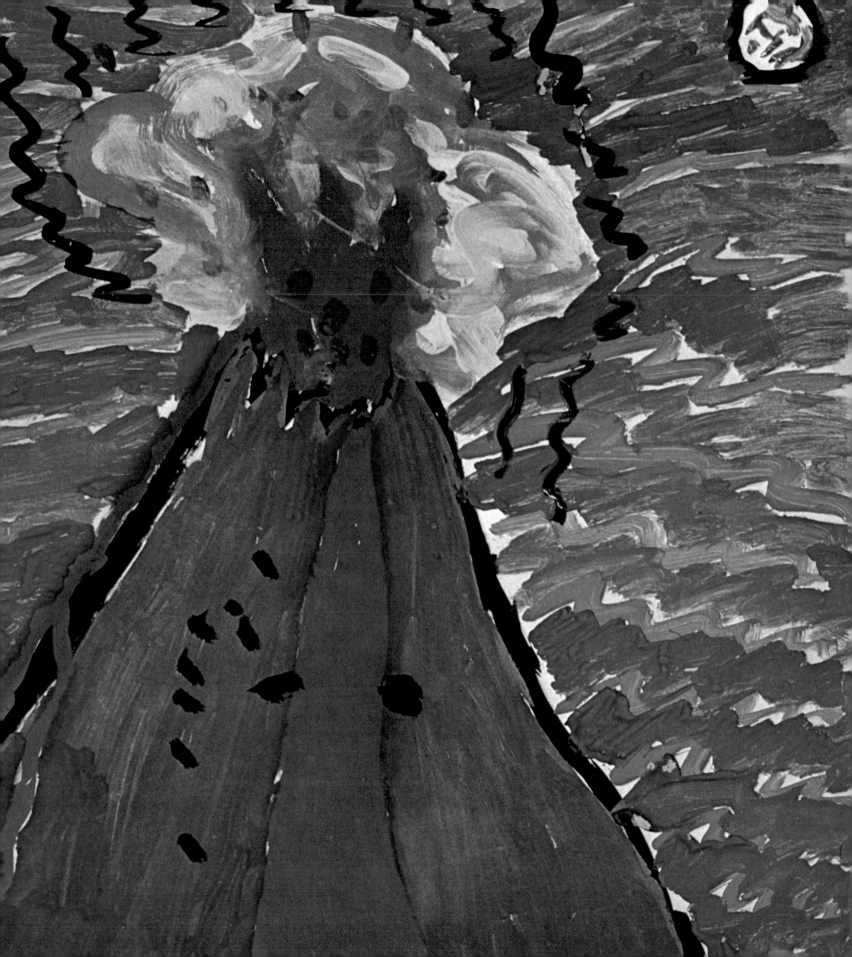

Oahu started out as two separate volcanoes, Waianae and Koolau. After a while, the two volcanoes joined together to make an island. Haleakala volcano made part of Maui. The island of Hawaii is five great volcanoes: Kohala, Mauna Kea, Hualalai, Mauna Loa and Kilauea. In all, the volcanoes made eight islands. These are the names of the islands in order of size: Hawaii, Maui, Oahu, Kauai, Molokai, Lanai, Niihau and Kahoolawe.

As soon as the first volcanoes of Hawaii stopped erupting, they began to be washed away by rain and ocean waves. Rain shaped the islands into hills and valleys. Many waves cut into the sides of the mountains to make cliffs. The surfaces were rough at first but they got smoothed by erosion. The rain made waterfalls. It also made dirt from crumbling lava. It took millions and millions of years for the lava to turn into sand and dirt. Nothing can grow on lava before it changes into sand and dirt. There were no coconut trees and no hibiscus flowers. The mountains and valleys were not that beautiful. The islands were just bare.

BORN IN FIRE

The sun was setting and the birds were still in the orange sky. The sun was gone and left the darkness. Suddenly a shooting fire flew up and brightened the earth. It was a volcano getting ready to born a new land. The red molten rock flew up in the sky and came down like a falling rain. It lasted all night and in the morning and the shooting power of the volcano never rest. The fire roar and the smoke became thicker and the lava piled higher. Days after days and nights after nights the restless volcano grew higher and higher. The lava rolled out to the ocean making smokes. Then the volcano was starting to get old. It didn't have enough power to shoot out the lava. Soon the volcano was dead and the land was part of the Hawaiian Islands. It was called Diamond Head.

HOW PLANTS AND ANIMALS CAME

The first plants had to come a long way to get here. They were probably ferns and mosses because their spores could float long distances in the air. Spores are smaller than seeds and can float like dust. As time kept going on, the slopes of the islands were covered with green and brown plants.

Under water, many little animals called coral clung to the shore. There the tiny animals lived, died and left little skeletons. They hardened and formed coral reefs. Fishes made homes in the reef.

A few birds found their way to the islands, probably lost or blown off course. That's how the nene goose and koloa duck got here. Insects like flies and beetles were blown to Hawaii on strong winds. Butterflies and bees flew to Hawaii. But very few animals really made it here. They would of had a little chance of making such a long trip.

Some birds that had eaten seeds came to this island. When they made shishi the seeds came out. It rained and the seeds grew into plants. Or the birds could of had seeds stuck in their feathers. The seeds could have fallen off and started to grow trees. Or maybe the seeds stuck to the birds' legs and, being picked off when they came to shore , it gets planted. It grows into a flower. The flower has a seed. It gets planted. Until the whole island has plants.

Some other seeds managed to get here on the ocean. Its current could take things many miles. One of these things is a hala seed. Hala trees grow on all island shores. Another way seeds could have got across the ocean is by being on branches that would float up on shore. One day, probably, a log came drifting by. On the log, lizards, spiders and bugs stayed. Some other animals on the log might be sand crabs.

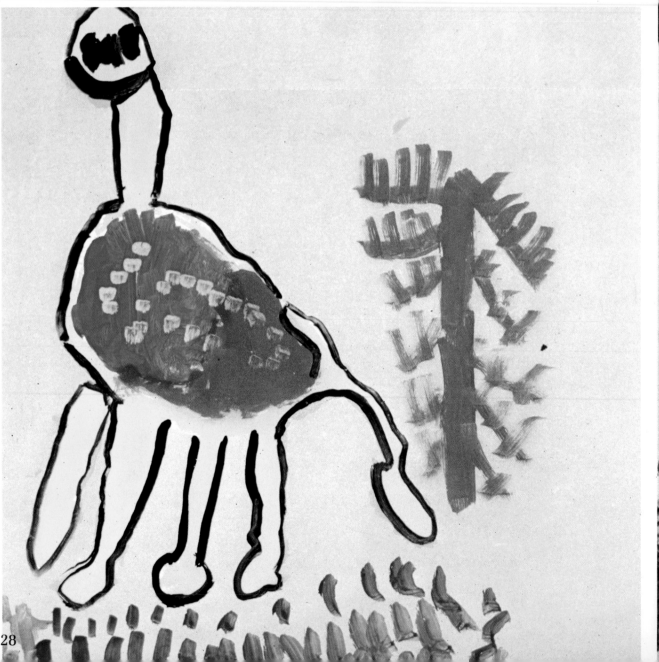

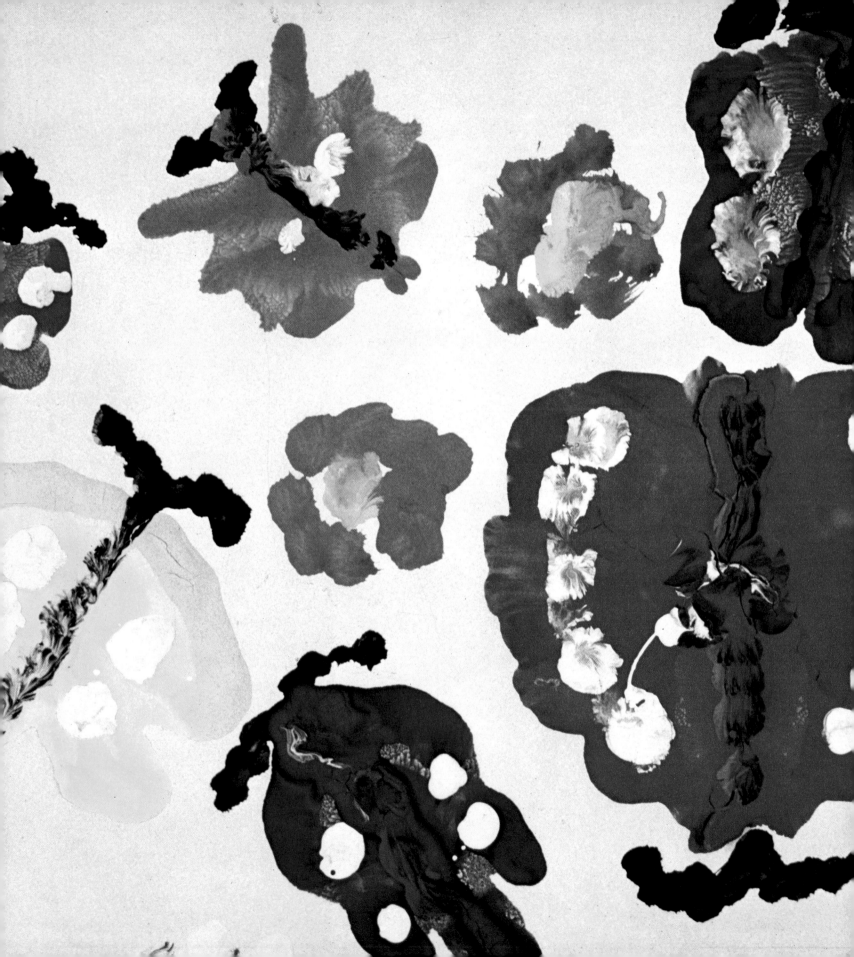

Then trees were growing, flowers were blooming and birds were eating fishes and making nests. The mountains and valleys looked more beautiful. Would you ever want it to look better in your life? But there were no people. All was quiet. Years passed and still the volcano didn't make a noise. It was a lonely island.

VOYAGE
TO HAWAII

Way far out from these islands there were other islands in the South Pacific called Polynesia. We know the Hawaiians are a branch of this great Polynesian family. But why the first settlers came to Hawaii is a mystery. Maybe, one day some fishermen went out from an island. There was a big storm and it blew them off course. After sailing a long time, they came upon Hawaii. People kept coming for long periods of time. Why? Maybe, fights went on and off in Polynesia. Some got out-fought so the ruling chief made them go to another island and they came to Hawaii. Maybe, some people went to Hawaii to search for a better place to live and bring up their children?

They at least traveled 2,000 miles. They didn't have compasses. Their map was the sun, birds, fish, stars and the moon. The voyager had to know about the waves and ocean currents. There were more people come but they got lost in the ocean somewhere. Some got lost from storms. Others got lost by whales that tipped them over and smashed them. Some got dead from no food to eat on their trip. But the ones who made it started a new life in Hawaii.

An old Hawaiian song says that the leader of the first voyage was Hawaii Loa. One day he thought about finding a new home. He sent his men into the forest with stone axes to cut down trees and make a double canoe. First they cut the branches off, then they shaped the sides and cut out the middle so you can sit in it. The women wove mat sails out of hala leaves. Then they tied the parts together with sennit rope.

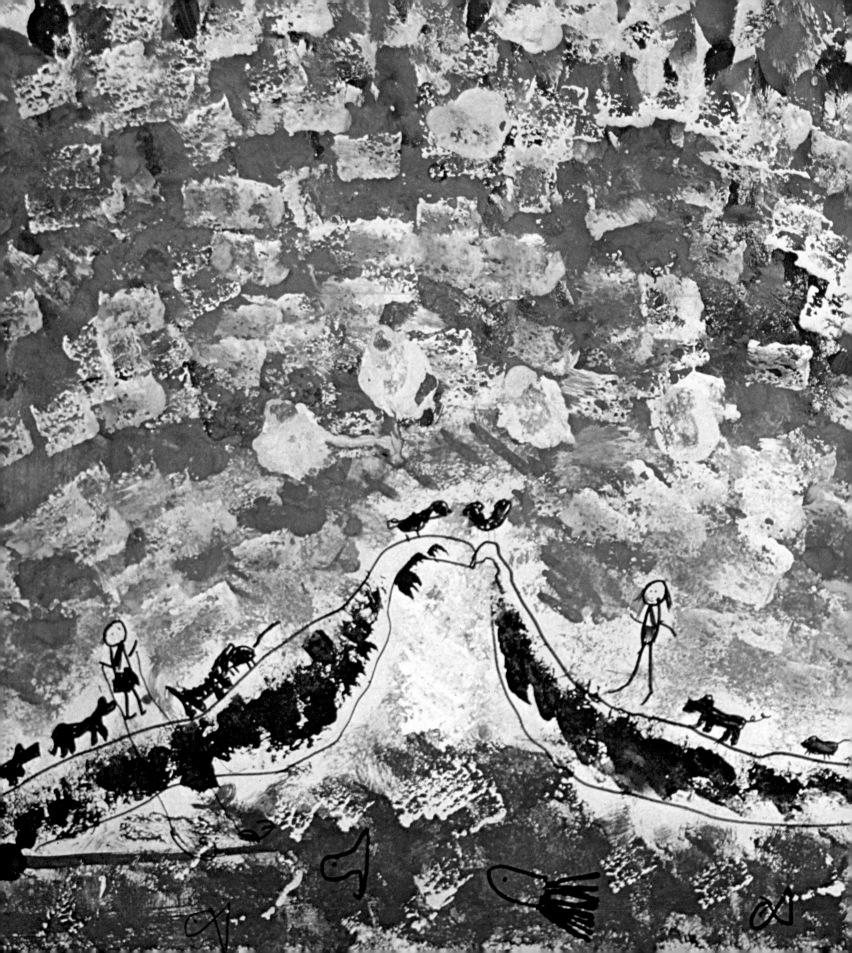

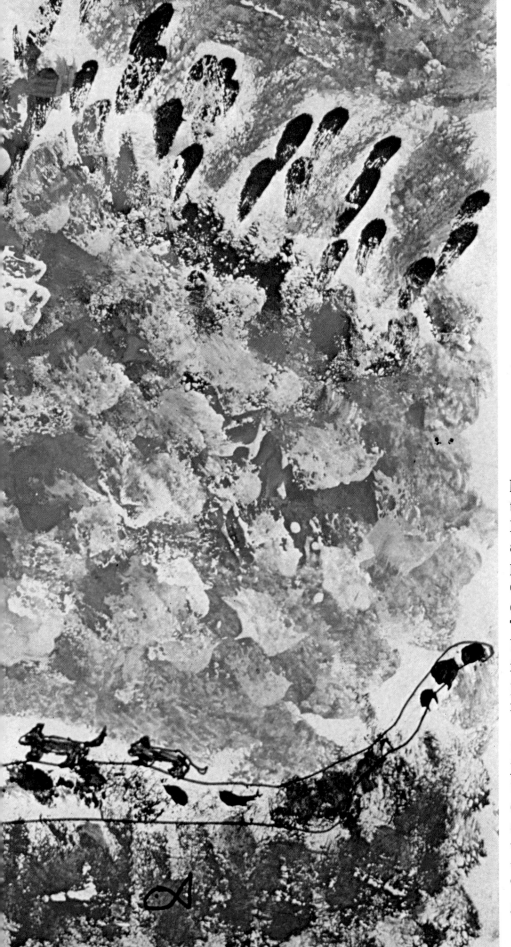

They made the double canoe so big it held more than 50 people. There was a little grass shack on a platform in the middle. In the canoes they put cages to hold dogs and some pigs and chickens. While the people were sleeping, rats got aboard the canoe. The Polynesians loaded water in coconut jugs, gourds and bamboo jars. They packed the canoe with taro and breadfruit to eat. They brought plants and fruits to grow in their new island. Some of these are breadfruit, coconuts, sugar cane, mountain apples, ti, banana and taro.

Just before they were going to leave, they prayed to their gods for a safe journey. Across the foamy blue waters of the Pacific the brave people of Polynesia came, bringing with them few supplies and a lot of courage. A Hawaiian navigator would have to know every star and planet visible to the eye to be able to set a course. They had to paddle and paddle until they got tired. The wind blew the sail.

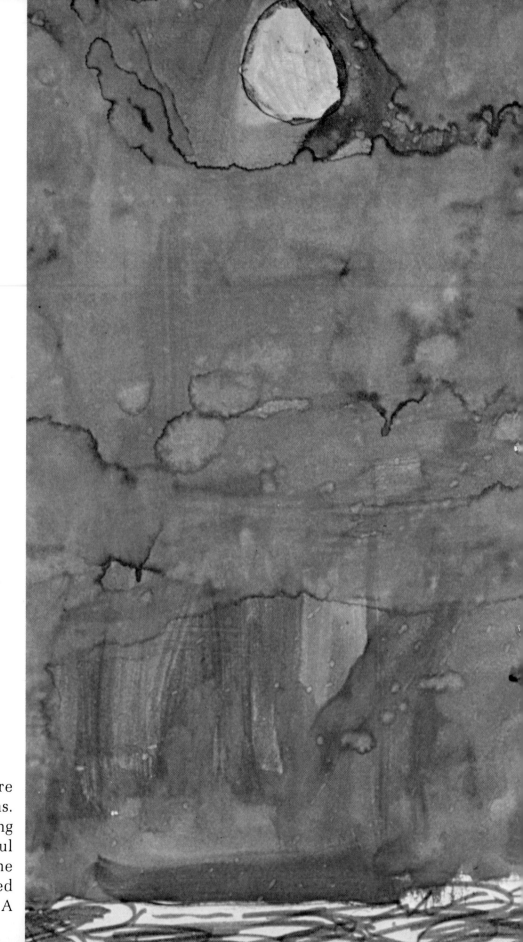

The days were passing. The pigs were making noise and so were the chickens. Then it got dark. The moon was shining bright. The waves were making beautiful sounds. For a month they traveled over the ocean still not finding land. They fished for food. Women cooked the fish. A

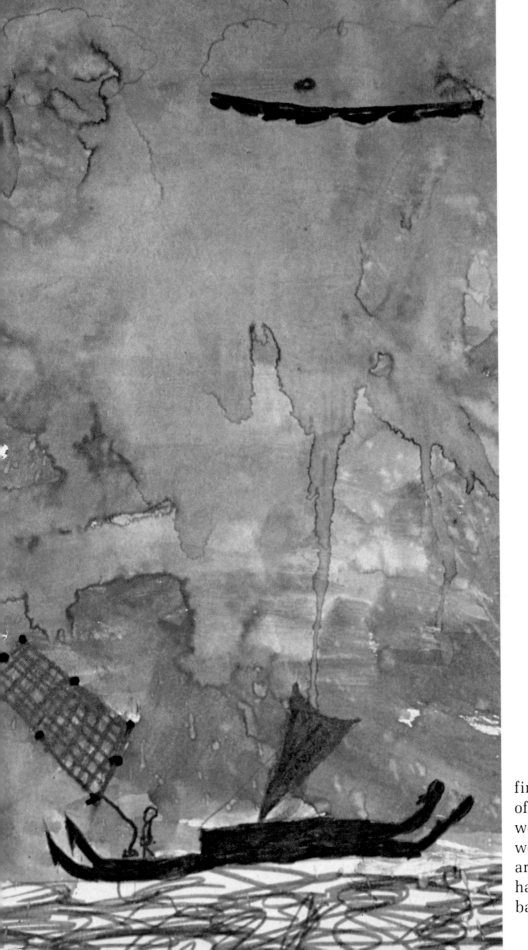

fireplace was made in the canoe on a bed of sand. Firewood was taken along. If you were a boy or a girl on the voyage, you would of been getting tired of being tossed around on the canoe. You would of worked hard, too, scooping water and throwing it back to the sea.

One day a watchman cried, "Look! There's land!" Everyone was shouting they were so happy. When the canoe stopped, they landed on the island and thanked the gods for a safe journey. After the people blessed the gods, they had to find food and water. They made their shacks. They finally finished the work, then took a rest. When they woke up, they had a party.

WHAT THEY DID FOR LIFE IN HAWAII

The early Hawaiians worked hard and really seemed to care for each other. Some were farmers, fishermen, house builders, canoe builders, adz makers, bird catchers and slaves. They dwelt close to nature and were a healthy, robust, intelligent and good-tempered folk. Men were called kanes. They and the boys farmed and went out in canoes to catch fish. The women were called wahines. They watched the children, took care of the house and made the clothes. Their husbands cooked the food. Fat people were considered beautiful. Most people were thin because there wasn't that much food.

Proud chiefs ruled those early people. The chiefs made strict laws which everybody had to follow. Some were sensible rules. There were other silly rules like the one that men and women could not eat together and one that said a man could be killed if he let his shadow fall on a chief.

Plants were very useful to the Hawaiians. One of these plants was ti. Hawaiians made sandals out of ti leaves. They made ti leaf capes for protection from rain. A children's delight was when they baked the root. It was their candy. One of the most useful plants was the coconut. Early Hawaiians ate the meat, drank the coconut milk and used the shell for containers. The leaves were used for building shelters and the husk for braiding sennit. Kukui nuts could be roasted and eaten. The oil was burned in lamps. Tapa cloth was made from strips of wauke bark and soaked and beaten. Taro was the main food. Another plant the Hawaiians used was the hala. They ate the sweet fruit and made mats out of the leaves. Plants were so important to the Hawaiians that they could not live without them.

For clothing the Hawaiian women wore skirts made of tapa around their waists. The skirts are called pa'u. The men wore a tapa cloth around their waists and legs called malo. Children wore the same. Important people such as chiefs wore feathered cloaks and helmets. Hula dancers dressed in different kinds of leis and wore flowers in their hair. They used dog teeth for leg ornaments.

When the first Hawaiians came they probably lived in caves before they built their houses which they called hale. The location of a hale was often chosen by the help of a kahuna, a wise priest. There were many kinds of superstitions to a hale. For instance, to build a hale near a heiau or fronting a cliff meant death to the family of that hale. Poles for the frame were cut and trimmed in the woods and then dragged to where the hale would be. Then people gathered the thatching materials

which were pili grass or hala leaves. The frame was tied together with sennit since there were no nails until the white man brought them. Later, pili grass was tied on for roof covering and the walls. The people put small pebbles to cover the dirt on the ground. Then they wove hala mats which were put down for floors. It was dark inside a hale because they did not have windows.

One of the ancient Hawaiian pastimes was surfing. There were many things to do.

Here's one. It is called pala'ie. It's a stick about 12 inches long with a loop at the end and you try to get a ball through the hoop. Older people played konane checkers and ulu maika. That is a game where you pound two pegs in the ground. Then each of the opponents rolls stones through the pegs. This is a game like bowling. Some of the games were like war: spear throwing, spear thrusting, wrestling and boxing. The Hawaiians were as warlike as any other branch of the Polynesians.

The stone adz was the principle cutting tool of the Hawaiians. Adz makers were members of a skilled profession. They searched for hard rocks which could be shattered into long fragments with the aid of a hammer stone. These fragments they chipped into rough adz forms. Finally, the adzes were smoothed by the aid of sand and water on a grindstone. Small adz blades were sometimes made of shell.

Rules Hawaiians lived by were called kapus. Special men called kahunas saw to it that the kapus were properly observed. the kahunas were very important men. They were priests, doctors and advisors to the king. Because the early Hawaiians could not write, they depended on the kahunas to remember the knowledge and teach it to young men and women. One of the most skillful kinds of kahuna was the kahuna lapa'au. He knew how to treat illnesses, how to set broken bones and how to use natural products to make medicines. There are nearly 200 kinds of plants and seaweed that the kahuna lapa'au used for his medicines. For example, the toothache would be healed by the root of the pua-kala plant that grows in sunny places along mountain roads.

THE GOD
THAT WASN'T REAL

On January 18, 1778, the people on Oahu saw a strange sight upon the ocean. It was two English ships. Their commander was Captain James Cook, the first white man to discover Hawaii. He sailed to Kauai and Niihau to trade nails and iron for food and water. His ships names were Resolution and Discovery. Captain Cook had a friend named Earl of Sandwich and that's how the Hawaiian Islands got to be called the Sandwich Islands. He sailed on to look for a river across America.

In 1779, Captain Cook returned to Hawaii and landed at Kealakekua Bay on the Big Island. All the people were full of joy. They sailed and paddled out to Captain Cook's ships in canoes. So many swam out they looked like schools of fish. Captain Cook and his men had never seen so many people before. The sailors were crazy about the women.

56

The natives thought Captain Cook was the god Lono who had promised to return to Hawaii on a floating island. They offered him many gifts and food every day. Captain Cook was the first haole to eat poi. His men said hello to the girls and took them for a walk. The Hawaiian men got mad but they did no harm. Captain Cook stayed two weeks. By the time he sailed away, the natives suffered a great loss of food.

Then a big storm came and Captain Cook had to go back. When the Polynesians saw him coming, they said, "Oh, no, not again!" A chief said, "If he is a god, he could go through a storm. So how do we know if he is a god?" But another chief said, "He looks like a god and acts like a god. Maybe, he really is. I'm not going to fool around."

One night the Hawaiians took one of Captain Cook's boats because they wanted the nails to use for fish hooks. The Hawaiians really wanted iron. When Captain Cook just noticed that his boat was gone, he tried to take one of the Hawaiian chiefs so he could say, "You better give me back my boat or I'll keep your chief."

Then they had a fight. A Hawaiian stabbed Captain Cook with a dagger. They took his head. Some took his legs and hands. To the Hawaiians, if you take a bone from a great man, you will become strong.

Today a monument marks the spot where Captain Cook fell. He will always be the man who made Hawaii known to the rest of the world even if he wasn't a god. After him, many other explorers and traders came to Hawaii.

HE WAS
A GOOD KING

In 1758, before Captain Cook came, a baby had been born to an alii woman on Hawaii. A kahuna told his mother he was going to be a great leader. The baby's uncle heard about it and got jealous. His mother thought the uncle might kill the baby so she gave him to a friend who took him to a valley where there were caves to hide. The baby was called Kamehameha which means, "the lonely one." That is because he had no one to play with.

61

When Kamehameha was five years old, another uncle took him to his village. This uncle taught him how to use spears, daggers, how to throw rocks, how to fight and all kinds of stuff like that. By the time Captain Cook came, Kamehameha had grown up to be a very tall man. The color of his skin was dark brown. One of Kamehameha's uncles was king. When the king died he gave Kamehameha's cousin, Kiwalao, the job of being king. Kamehameha got the job of keeping care of the war god, Kukailimoku. The king died and the cousins got into a war about who was going to get the land. Kiwalao was killed.

Kamehameha prayed to the war god that one king should rule over all the islands. The war god agreed. So Kamehameha thought about it and decided to become king. His soldiers sharpened their spears and daggers and got rocks to throw and guns from white men. In 1790 Kamehameha defeated the chief of Maui, Kahekili, at the battle of Iao Valley. He went to Oahu in 1795. A long line of canoes landed on the shore from the present Waialae golf course to Waikiki. Kamehameha then grouped his warriors up for the attack. The battle took place in Nuuanu Valley to the very edge of the Pali. Many of the opposing warriors met their deaths by being pushed off. Kamehameha was going to Kauai but his canoe started to sink in a storm and he couldn't get to Kauai. But the chief on Kauai gave up anyway and Kamehameha was king of all the islands.

He was a good king to his people. Under him the Hawaiians had food, animals and clothes. He went out in the field and started to grow taro. The people said, "I will go out and help him." After they were finished, they went out and got some fish. They were healthy again. More white men came. Don Francisco de Paula Marin, a Spanish settler, brought pineapples. Kamehameha sent great quantities of sandalwood to China to get money He led his nation through its first contact with people and ideas from the rest of the world.

Days went past and King Kamehameha died in 1819. His body was taken to a concealed cave and to this day no one knows where he is buried. Now we called him Kamehameha the Great.

HOW THE KAPUS GOT BROKEN

King Kamehameha had a son named Liholiho. After Liholiho's father died, Liholiho became King Kamehameha II. The people were worried because they thought Liholiho wouldn't be as good as his father in leading. He was 22 years old. He had curly hair. He was tall and had lighter skin than his father. Liholiho was heavy built. He looked handsome in a uniform like the white men wore.

Liholiho and his father's favorite wife ruled Hawaii together. Her name was Kaahumanu. She did not like the kapus because one of the kapus was that women couldn't eat with the men. Also, the men got the best food. Kaahumanu had learned that there was no such thing in other lands. She wanted Liholiho to do something about it. Liholiho's wife did not like kapus.

One day Liholiho gave a luau at his grass palace in Kailua, Kona. The men sat at the big table and the women by the small table. Liholiho came out of his seat and sat with the women. When the people saw, they were shocked. They thought the gods would send down lightning. But nothing happened. The news spread island to island. Women ate with the men and men ate with the women. Other kapus were broken, like when the chief passed people did not fall on the ground. The kapu sticks did not stand anymore. Heiaus were torn down.

Traders swarmed around the chiefs, trading tools and iron for sandalwood. Men and women had to carry sandalwood down the mountains on their heads. There was no time to grow crops. After a few years of this all the sandalwood was gone. Honolulu became a noisy place because sailors came and went whaling. The harbor was filled with ships. Streets were filled with sailors and traders.

The king learned from the white men the ways they lived. He was the first king to travel from Hawaii. Liholiho and his queen visited the king and queen of England. They caught the measles and died there. So they shipped his body back and buried him. His brother became king.

COMING OF THE LONG NECKS

Many Hawaiians followed the traders to America. One of these Hawaiians was a sixteen year-old orphan boy named Opukahaia. In 1808 he had swum out to an American ship anchored in Kealakekua Bay and begged the captain to take him along. The captain took Opukahaia to his home in New Haven, Connecticut. The boy was very smart and learned fast. He was received into the Christian faith.

Opukahaia told the people of New England that missionaries should be sent to Hawaii to teach his people. But he died of typhus before the missionaries started out in 1819. They came on the small brig Thaddeus. The Thaddeus carried two ministers, two teachers, a doctor, a printer and a farmer. Their leader was the Rev. Hiram Bingham. The farmer had a wife and five children. All the other men just had wives. It took these people five months to reach Hawaii.

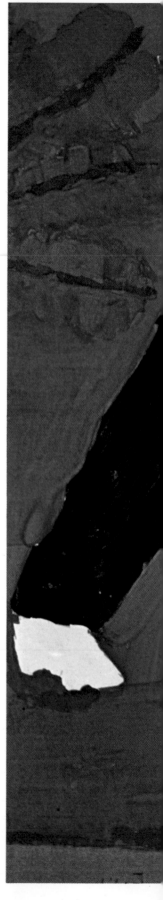

On March 30, 1820, they sighted Mauna Kea. They landed at Kailua on Hawaii. There was an argument about whether they could stay. The king said, "You may stay for one year, then I will decide if you can stay forever." The missionaries brought along many cases, bags, boxes, chests and lumber for a house. Missionary men wore coats and trousers and shirts. The women wore calico dresses. Hawaiians called the lady missionaries Long Necks because they wore clothes up to their necks.

When the missionaries landed in Honolulu, they lived in grass houses. The first thing they did was to make the king and queen be their friends so if they wanted something changed the king would change it. The first thing they wanted changed was that the Hawaiians had hardly any clothes on. Women didn't wear any tops. Missionaries talked with the king about this matter and the king agreed that women should wear tops. The Long Necks taught the Hawaiian women how to make muumuus.

Pretty soon the missionaries built churches and schools and started to teach the Hawaiians to read and write. The missionaries made books with a machine called the printing press. Hawaiians thought it was a magic machine. The first book the missionaries made was a primer. There were so few copies of the primer at first that the Hawaiians had to take turns studying. They learned to read the alphabet upside down and sideways and backwards while they were sitting around the person holding the primer waiting for their turn. The missionaries were very helpful to the Hawaiians trying their best to help them.

After a year, the king said, "You may stay and build your wooden house." It was the first wooden house in Hawaii. The house had small window panes and a deep cellar. When it was done they whitewashed the walls. They called it the Frame House. You can still visit it in the center of Honolulu.

THE WISE KING

There was a prince who was very sad when King Kamehameha II died. He never even made one smile. His name was Kauikeaouli and he was Kamehameha II's little brother. He was eleven years old when he became Kamehameha III. Until he got to be eighteen years old, Kaahumanu ruled for him. In 1833 Kamehameha III started being king for himself. A council of chiefs made laws.

Kamehameha III was a wise king and a very kind man. But the Hawaiian Islands were changing fast. Many haoles came. More missionaries came. Other men came to go whaling. Whaling stores started. The king had to make new rules for these people. To help, the missionaries started a school for children of Hawaiian royalty in 1839. It was called the Royal School. At the school the children were taught to read, write, and do arithmetic. They were also taught about Christ and each child was given a Christian name. A missionary began to teach Kamehameha III about laws. Hawaii got its first constitution in 1840. Punahou School started in 1842.

In 1843 the British people that came to Hawaii got in a grumble. A British warship came and took over Hawaii for six months. The British lowered the Hawaiian flag and highered the English flag. The streets were changed to English names. The Hawaiian people were wondering what happened. Then in July a British admiral named Richard Thomas came in a bigger ship and gave back the land. The Hawaiian flag was raised again. There were shouts of joy! On that day, the king said, "Ua mau ke ea o ka aina i ka pono" (The life of the land is perpetuated in righteousness). Hawaii was independent again.

Another thing that Kamehameha III did was give land to the Hawaiian people. This was called the Great Mahele. Before, the king had all the land. Now one-third was for the king, one-third for the chiefs, and one-third for the people who lived and worked on the land. Kamehameha III died in 1854. He was king for 30 years. He gave the people rights and he gave the people land.

WHALING

As Kamehameha III began his reign, whaling had replaced sandalwood trade to make money in Hawaii. The first whale ship came to Hawaii in 1819. Then more and more came. They made regular visits to Hawaii where they could get fresh water and food. This brought money to the Islands.

The ships stayed until they were filled. Then they went back into the ocean and started to catch whales again. When they saw a school of whales they put small boats in the water and tried to get close enough to spear it. Sometimes the whales knocked a boat over with their tails. Sometimes it was a hard trip because it stormed and the sea was rough. People on board the ships had to wait for months until they caught a lot of whales.

Lahaina was the whaling capitol of Hawaii. The seamen brought diseases and disorder to the native population. Then people found better things to use than whale oil and whale bone. Whaling began to decline in the 1860's. Now there is no whaling in the Islands.

KING
KAMEHAMEHA IV

NO MORE KAMEHAMEHAS

King Kamehameha III did not have any children when he died. He had adopted his nephew, Alexander Liholiho, grandson of Kamehameha I. Alexander got to be Kamehameha IV in 1855. He was 20 years old, tall and handsome. The people thought he had a quick temper. But he turned out to be a good king.

Alexander was educated. Once, when he was younger, he and his brother took a trip to England and the United States. They went to Royal School. There Alexander met Emma Rooke, one of the most beautiful women in Hawaii. The new king married Emma who was to be queen. The people liked them because they were kind and very nice together.

During this time, people in Hawaii began to grow sugar cane and coffee beans. Chinese came to work in the fields. Hawaiian people were dying of diseases that were brought on ships. There was no place for the people to get well. Because the king and queen loved the people so much, they collected money to make a hospital. The king went from door to door. The queen helped. In 1859 they had enough money to start Queen's Hospital.

Three years after they got married, Alexander and Emma had a baby. It was a boy that brought joy and happies to the people. But when the boy was only four years old, he got sick and died. King Kamehameha IV lost faith in being king because he loved his son so much. He was not interested in the government. When he was 29 years old, the king died of heart broke. His wife died of old age.

The king forgot to name someone to be king of his lands after him. So Kamehameha IV's brother, Lot, became King Kamehameha V. He was educated like his brother. And he was firm. When he said, "Jump," the people jumped because they respected him. He wasn't married.

During the time Kamehameha V was king, the whaling industry died. Sugar became bigger and rice became a big crop and coffee was also popular. These crops got to be Hawaii's main business because people shipped and sold them all over the world. The first steamship service to Hawaii from the United States started in 1867. The ships ran by wood burning and took mail to the islands. About this time a man named Mark Twain came to the Hawaiian Islands. He's the one who made the book, "Huckleberry Finn." He wrote this about Hawaii, "The loveliest fleet of islands that lies anchored in any ocean."

While Kamehameha V was king, some Hawaiian people got a real bad disease called leprosy. The king built a leprosy colony for the people and it is still there on Molokai. Father Damien was a Catholic priest who went to Molokai with all the lepers. He was horrified. Father Damien got the government to help more. Some lepers helped him build a church. Later, Father Damien caught leprosy himself and died in 1889. A statue of him was put in the State Capitol.

Kamehameha V died in 1872. He was king only nine years. But in those nine years he did a lot of things for his people. When he died there were no more Kamehamehas to be king.

KING FOR ONLY ONE YEAR

For several weeks after Kamehameha V died, Hawaii had no king. This had never happened before. For the first time the people could pick who they wanted to be king. There were two men who wanted to become king. They were William Lunalilo and David Kalakaua.

Lunalilo was a spoiled prince but he was kind to everyone. He did not want to fight or get into trouble. He went to the Royal School and he was a good student. A meeting was held by Lunalilo and he told the people two things they can count on. "If I am king I will promise that the constitution of King Kamehameha III will be back in Hawaii and I shall govern by the constitution." The people were pleased with Lunalilo's promises.

Kalakaua came from a noble family and he worked very well with the last king. One night he called a meeting of the boys. Kalakaua promised at that meeting to cut the taxes and put Hawaiians, not haoles, in public offices. Kalakaua was all for the Hawaiian people,but the people were not sure to believe him or not.

In 1873 on New Year's Day, Lunalilo was picked to be king. They picked him because they thought he was honest and fair and a fun person. And because they thought he could really do the job of being king. But he was king for only one year when he got real sick and died. He left his property and money to establish a home for poor Hawaiians. It is called Lunalilo Home.

HAWAII'S LAST KING

After Lunalilo died, the king makers went to work again. Some people wanted Queen Emma to rule. But other Hawaiians wanted a king, not a queen. Finally, the legislature met. It's men had been elected by the people. They made the choice and they picked David Kalakaua.

He was called the Merry Monarch because he was fat and healthy. Also because he liked to dance and hear music. Kalakaua's wife, Kapiolani, came from the Kamehameha family. With the introduction of foreign methods, the Hawaiian culture was slowly dying away. Kalakaua had become aware of this. He wanted to keep the ancient Hawaiian history and preserve the culture. So he brought back "kahunaism" and the hula, which had been stopped by the missionaries. He also brought back a lot of old chants and music. He built Iolani Palace.

When Kalakaua was elected king on February 12, 1874, the House of Representatives was also elected. Only native Hawaiians were voted in. It was the first time since 1851 that no haoles were elected. Some said the main cause of this was a growing prejudice against foreigners.

In 1874, Kalakaua went on a visit to Washington, D.C. for a couple of months. He was the first king from Hawaii to go to Washington. He was a guest of President Ulysses S. Grant. As a result of his visit, Kalakaua made an important treaty with the United States. Hawaii was allowed to send sugar, rice and coffee to the U.S. free of tax. In return, the U.S. was given the right to send things to Hawaii duty free.

The treaty influenced a lot of Hawaiian history. There was a big sugar boom. Twenty-five million pounds of sugar were shipped to the mainland in 1875. Because of the sugar boom, more roads, bridges, even railroads and telephones came to Hawaii. Many more people were needed to work in the fields and mills. Chinese, Portuguese and Japanese came to work in the plantations and that's why we have Chinese, Portuguese and Japanese people in Hawaii. The most important thing the treaty did was set up a relation to the United States which later led to the overthrow of the Hawaiian monarchy.

Later on, in 1881, Kalakaua took a trip around the world. No Hawaiian king had ever done this. So he decided to be the first one. He was the first Hawaiian king to visit Japan. After seeing so many foreign countries, King Kalakaua got new ideas about royal ceremonies. When he came back, he held a coronation ceremony to celebrate his ninth year as king. There was a big luau and many dances dedicated to him. He crowned himself king on a stage built on the Iolani Palace grounds especially for the coronation. Now it's called the bandstand.

When Kalakaua was elected he did the right things for a long time. Then he started to make mistakes. Scandal and corruption caused him to play less of a role as a king. In 1887 haole businessmen and sugar planters made him sign a constitution that took away some of the king's power. Kalakaua went to San Francisco on a vacation trip and died there in January 1891. He was Hawaii's last king.

King David Kalakaua, The Merry Monarch

THE SALT AIR
OF HEAVEN

Liliuokalani, whose name means "The Salt Air of Heaven," was the sister of Kalakaua. She had served twice already as Kalakaua's regent during his absence from Hawaii. On January 28, 1891, she ascended the throne at the age of fifty-two. Liliuokalani had studied at Royal School. She spoke Hawaiian and English very gracefully. Her husband was John Owen Dominis who died seven months after she took the throne.

The new queen had a strong will and wanted to come more strong. She demanded a new constitution that would give back power tooked away from her brother. That got her into a very big problem. They still had Hawaiians on the islands but there were more haoles come all the time. Americans controlled most of Hawaii's wealth. The haoles wanted to control Hawaii but the Hawaiians wanted Hawaii to become whatever they wanted Hawaii to become. Royalists in the legislature supported the queen to overthrow the constitution of 1887. Liliuokalani also wanted to appoint members of the upper house of the legislature instead of having them elected.

An Annexation Club formed as a secret organization of businessmen and sugar planters in Honolulu to have a more

stable government and to get Hawaii to be part of the United States. Its members were mostly of foreign blood. In 1893, after the queen had dismissed the legislature, she wanted to proclaim the new constitution. But her own cabinet was afraid to sign it for fear of a revolution. The queen agreed to change her mind but the promise came too late. All the important businessmen were against her already.

The times were very tense. A committee of members from the Annexation Club resolved not to have anymore kings and queens in Hawaii. Sanford B. Dole, son of an American missionary, took command of the recruits. Troops from the USS Boston in Honolulu harbor landed to protect American citizens and to keep order. The queen was defended by the police and her household guards. But the only shot fired during the revolution was by a Hawaiian policeman at a man driving an ammunition wagon.

Liliuokalani surrendered her powers under protest, yielding to the superior force of the United States. The committee proclaimed the ending of the monarchy and siezed government records. They established a provisional government until annexation could be arranged. The men from the Boston stayed ashore and on February 1, 1893 the Stars and Stripes were raised to show that Hawaii was under United States protection. Many Hawaiians cried.

The haole businessmen started a Republic in 1894 and elected Sanford Dole. They didn't call him king but instead they gave him a new name. They called

him president of the Hawaiian Islands. The new government punished Liliuokalani. They told her to stay in her own room at Washington Place for nine months and she couldn't go anyplace else. After this period passed, they forgave her and let her out. President Grover Cleveland tried in vain to restore Liliuokalani to her throne. Finally, the Hawaiian Islands became a Territory of the United States in 1898. This man, Sanford Dole, became the first governor of the new Territory.

Liliuokalani made two trips to the United States after she lost her throne. She is perhaps best known today for her song, "Aloha Oe," which became the traditional farewell song of Hawaii.

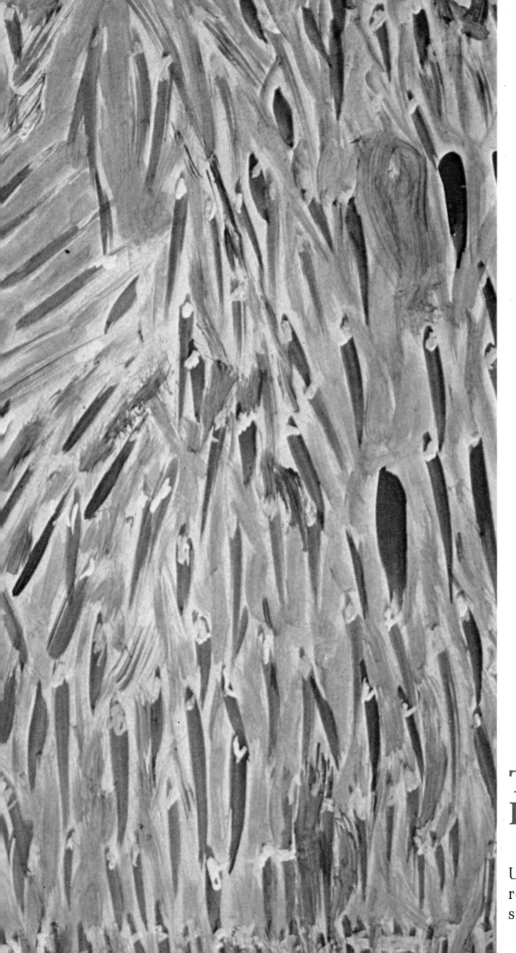

TREASURE IN THE FIELDS

After Hawaii became a part of the United States, more foreigners came. One reason was a treasure in the fields called sugar cane.

The early Polynesians brought sugar cane to the Islands. It looks a little like a stalk of corn. It grows almost ten feet high with a feathery tassel on top. It takes two years for the cane to grow up. Men come with long sticks with flaming cloth on the end. They burn the cane to get the leaves off. The fire is orange and so is the sky. Black smoke goes up. When the leaves are burned, the stalks are left. They are cut and big trucks take them to the sugar mill. At the mill, heavy rollers squeeze out the sweet juice. This is cooked to a thick syrup and dried to raw sugar which is shipped to the mainland of the United States to be refined.

Hawaiians grew sugar cane to chew like candy. In 1802, Chinese began to grow sugar cane on Lanai. By 1842 the Koloa Plantation on Kauai had a good mill and was producing good sugar. In 1848 the California gold rush was started.

At that time, the sugar plantations needed workers so they turned to China. In 1865, the Chinese migration really started. About 1878 the Portuguese were coming to Hawaii. The Japanese migration started in 1885. In 1909 the sugar plantations needed more workers so they got some from the Philippines.

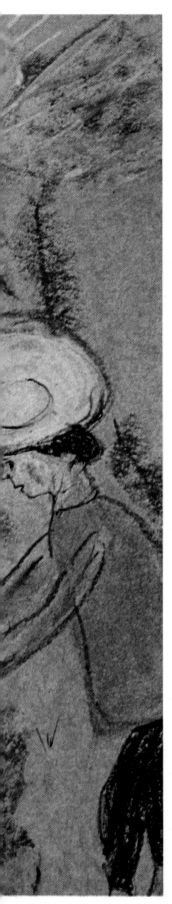

Another important industry in Hawaii got to be growing pineapples. The pineapple industry grew with the invention of the Ginaca machine in 1913. The Ginaca machine removes the shell and core in a single operation, leaving a smooth, clean cylinder of tender fruit.

By 1920, sugar was still Hawaii's number one industry. Pineapple was number two. Both industries required equipment such as tractors, trucks and harvesting machines. The Hawaiian Sugar Planters Association was formed to help figure out how to get workers from other places and how to grow cane better. Many insects attack the sugar cane plant. The sugar growers brought in natural insect enemies. By the 1930's, the sugar industry in Hawaii was famous for its research and modern methods.

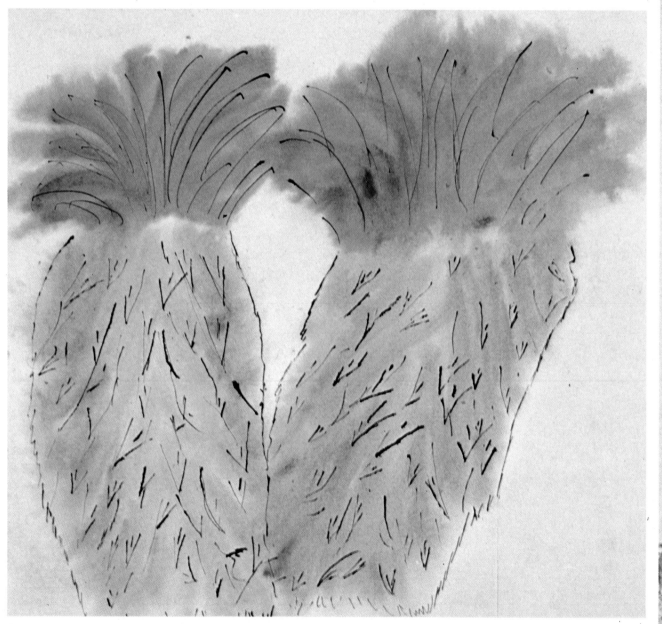

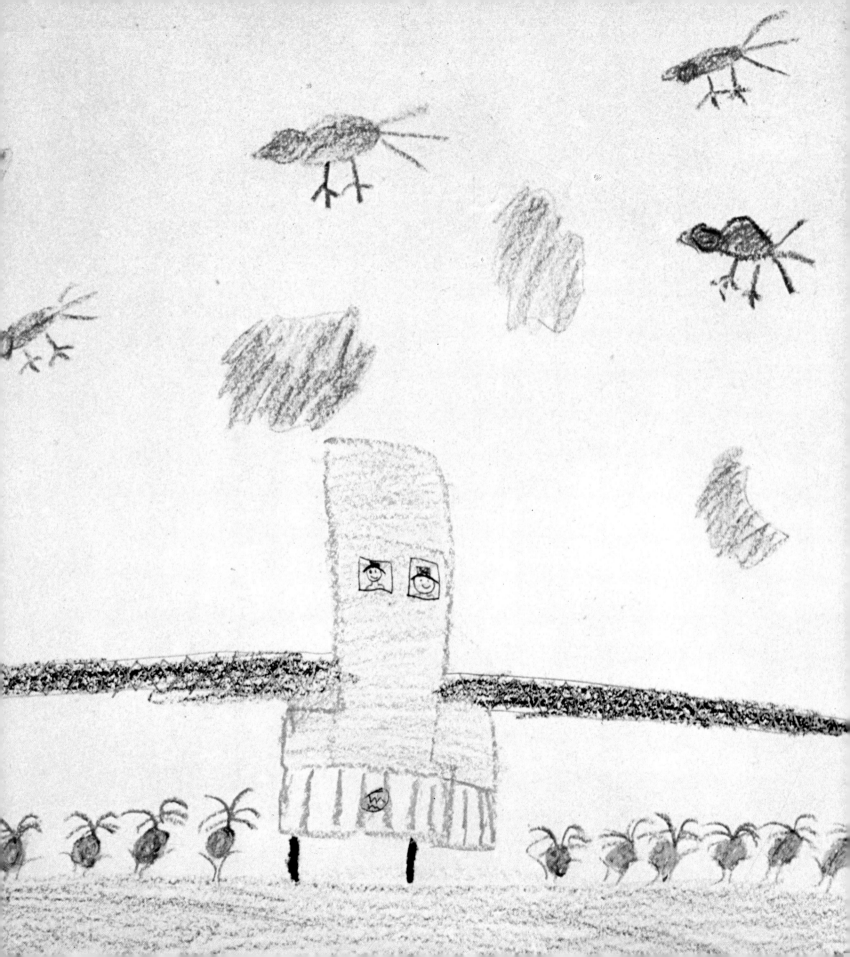

"DON'T YOU UNDERSTAND? THIS IS WAR!"

In 1887 King Kalakaua had given the United States a right to develop a naval coaling station at Pearl Harbor in return for a new treaty of reciprocity. The navy made an attempt to deepen the harbor in 1900. The first dry dock was built in 1919. By 1940, Pearl Harbor was America's biggest naval base in the Pacific. A surprise attack on Pearl Harbor on December 7, 1941 by Japanese planes pulled the United States into World War II.

The American fleet and army were not on wartime alert. At about 7:55 a.m. the first of 360 Japanese planes attacked army aircraft, Pacific Fleet ships and many other military installations nearby. The assault lasted two hours. During the attack, the Pacific Fleet lost some of their best ships. Some of these ships were the battleships Arizona, California, Oklahoma and West Virginia. Only three were able to sail again. All in all, 18 ships were sunk and 174 American planes were destroyed. Over 1,000 people were killed just in the Arizona. This was a crippling blow to Hawaii defenses. But Japanese planes had concentrated mostly on destroying planes and ships. They left the bases with repair facilities practically undamaged.

Many people in Hawaii remember that morning. A boy named Robert Nishiyama was attending the Chua Gakuen Church school. Suddenly, there was much noise, screams; walls and ceilings falling. Robert's second grade friend lay without an arm . This was from an anti-aircraft shell that went the wrong way.

Frances was with her 59-year-old grandmother on this sunny Sunday morning. The rest of the family had gone to the Aala Market for the weekly marketing. The telephone jangled. Aunty Florence who lived in Kailua cried over the phone to seven-year-old Frances to hide grandmother because she was a Japanese alien and all aliens were going to be taken away. Aunty continued, "Don't you understand? This is war! Turn on the radio!" What does war mean to a seven year-old?

Another girl was going to Sunday School in Honolulu but they had to come back because the FBI came and took the Buddhist minister away. They couldn't go to school either because the army took over the school. Their brand new radio was taken away so they couldn't listen to the news or music. After the war they got it back but it was not as good as it was before.

After World War II started, there was much hustle and bustle to be done. For instance, people had to put tarpaper on the windows. Then they dug trenches in their backyards. The trench had to contain food, water and medication. Many schools were used for civilian defense. Block wardens came around to see if there were any cracks in the tarpaper. Curfew was strictly enforced. Everyone had to be off the streets by 10 p.m. Many things were rationed and scarce. Such things were gas, silk, rubber products and alcoholic beverages. Eggs and butter wouldn't be fresh. The butter would be rancid. Along with these problems, everyone had to get three shots each year for tetanus, typhoid and flu.

At school all the children were instructed how to put on a gas mask. Everywhere you looked, you could see everyone preparing for war. Night and day you could hear ground drillers drilling and machinery digging. The army was building pill boxes. At night you could barely see the lights shine through the windows. Even the car headlights were painted black with a clear circle as big as a soda pop cap to give just enough light to identify a moving vehicle was on the road. As the siren went on, this was a signal for the town to be completely blacked out. How scary it was! You felt like a blind person because you saw only darkness as soon as everyone obeyed the siren.

Months went by. The pill boxes were finished. The war was getting worse. Headlines in the newspaper screamed war, war, war! Children couldn't play long after school because they had to be close to home all the time. Army, army, army, that's all everyone talked about. It seemed like the whole island became a military base.

Months went by with the war still on. Routine chores went on daily as usual. Finally, the United States dropped two atomic bombs on Hiroshima and Nagasaki and Japan gave up. The most wonderful words said on the radio were, "World War II has ended!" After four full years of drilling and darkness, everyone was so relieved that they all switched clothes and danced in the streets until the next day. The church bells rang, car horns were tooting and you could hear people laughing for everyone was so happy. At night the town lights shone brightly. No more sirens, no more blackouts, no more fears were with us anymore.

Today there is a memorial of the USS Arizona in the middle of Pearl Harbor. It reminds us of those sailors and soldiers who have given their lives to let us live our lives and enjoy our islands.

DANCING IN THE STREETS

As a Territory, Hawaii could elect a delegate to the U.S. Congress who would represent them but who had no vote. People in Hawaii paid taxes to the Federal government but could not vote on how the money was spent. Hawaii voters elected fifteen Senators and thirty Representatives to their own legislature. But the President of the United States appointed the Governor of Hawaii and other officials. Hawaii was a Territory like this for fifty-nine years.

The people of Hawaii, except for a few, wanted the Islands to be a state of the United States so they could elect their own governor and congressmen. Some congressmen in Washington did not want this because Hawaii is the only state that does not lie in the mainland of North America. Also, in Hawaii there are many people of other races: Hawaiians, Japanese, Filipinos, Chinese, Koreans and others.

Another problem was that Alaska was being considered to be a state at the same time. Hawaii was mostly Republican so Democrats in Congress voted against Hawaii. Alaska was mostly Democrat so Republicans in Congress voted against Alaska. Neither one was getting to be a state. Hawaii Delegate John A. Burns said, "Let Alaska go first. Then Hawaii can get in later on." Alaska went first.

In August, 1959, Hawaii became a state. The newspaper boy was selling newspapers with a picture of President Dwight D. Eisenhower signing the paper. There were hula girls dancing in the streets. Cars had to stop. All the people were celebrating. They made luaus and a bonfire.

After statehood, Hawaii started to boom. Lots of money and new companies came in. These companies brought money and employment. More people came to Hawaii. Real estate was increasing in development and prices. More motor vehicles were being brought over and registered. More hotels were opening in Waikiki and all around.

The people picked the hibiscus as the state flower. The state bird is the nene, a Hawaiian goose. The kukui, state tree, has long, spreading branches with light green leaves. It is found on mountain slopes and may grow up to sixty feet high. Hawaii's state flag was designed way back in the early 1800's. It is a combination of the Union Jack of Great Britain and the American Flag. The Jack represents Kamehameha's friendship for Britain. The eight red, white and blue stripes represent the eight major islands in Hawaii.

SOFT GREEN GRASS AND SOMETIMES A BAND

Hawaii has changed a whole lot from ti leaf skirts to miniskirts. Some things we have nowadays are television, cars, jets, airplanes, movies, schools, tall buildings, restaurants, clocks and many others. Today is better in some ways. Like now we have doctors and hospitals. But we have a lot of smoke, too, and the smoke pollutes the air. Hawaii now has a booming economy. Almost any kind of jobs can be found, airline pilot to zoologist, there are jobs.

The population of Hawaii is growing. Each year, many babies are born and people move in which makes Oahu a crowded place. The people of Hawaii are of many different backgrounds. Some are African, Caucasian, Filipino, Portuguese, Hawaiian, Indian, Japanese, Chinese and more. These races cooperate together but sometimes they think prejudice about each other. Hawaii has many schools and colleges. Some of these have their own football, baseball and basketball teams. The most popular of these colleges is the University of Hawaii. Some people go to school barefoot. At the schools there are rules. Some people break the rules and get sent to the office.

107

Honolulu has lots of buildings and stores all close to each other. There are so many automobiles that your car can't go very fast. People from the city think the city is best but the country people think that the country is best where you can stretch out. In the country there is ginger and plumeria and hibiscus and many beaches. Also sugar cane.

In Hawaii there are all kinds of foods. One of these is poi, a sticky substance that tastes like wall-paper paste to malihinis. There are also bananas, mangos, guavas, coconuts, lilikoi, papaya and taro grown in Hawaii. Many fish are caught off the coast. The most popular is mahimahi.

Hawaii has beautiful beach parks and recreational areas. In the beaches there is soft sand, clean water and lavatories. In the parks there are big trees, soft green grass and sometimes a band is playing. All those beautiful things bring tourists which is good for Hawaii. But with the tourists, that means more cars and more accidents. Also with more tourists, that brings up our population. This causes more crime. These are some of the problems Hawaii has now.

THINGS
TO SEE AND DO

Hawaii is good for vacations because there are a lot of scenic places as you go around the islands. You can relax while enjoying the climate. There are swaying palm trees, noisy mynah birds and rainbows. The sunsets are like the heavens opening up. You never get tired of watching the birds gliding over the ocean.

Lots of people like to go to Waikiki. There is a big wall going into the ocean where kids jump off into the water. You can surf because there are waves. Some kids like to sit on the beach and watch the people. Waikiki has a hotel in which there is a glass elevator where you can see all over from it. In the hotel there are shows on the stage you can go to see. There are lots of tall buildings in Waikiki. At night, when the lights are on, it looks very nice.

In Honolulu there is old Iolani Palace, built by Hawaii's last king. It is the only palace in the United States. If you hike up into Manoa Falls behind Honolulu there are seven waterfalls you can see all flowing at once several times a year. Going around the island there is Diamond Head, then Sea Life Park where you learn about fish. On along there is the Polynesian Cultural Center which shows many things of long ago. You can also drive to Waimea

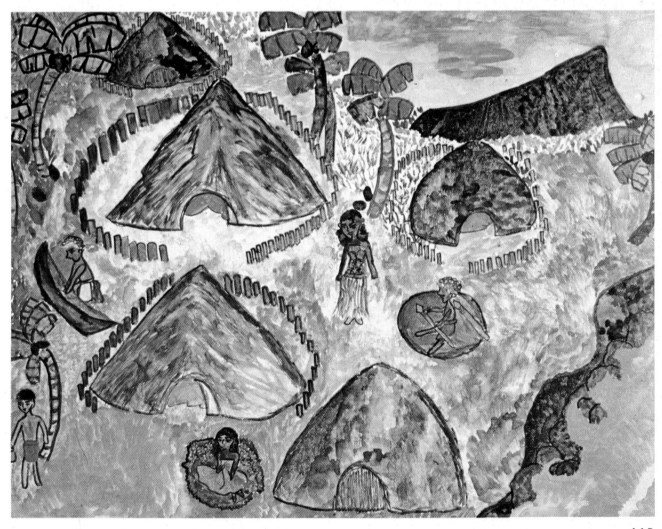

Falls, Nuuanu Pali and Pearl Harbor.

Hiking to Sacred Falls is really fun. It is on the other side of the island from Honolulu. The falls is in a steep canyon. There is a dirt road on the way up, and a parking place. The foot trail is about one and a half miles long. It is beautiful on the way, lots of trees and very shady. You won't be hot. The real things is the falls. There's a pool where you can dive off the rocks. The water is cold and deep. When it comes down the waterfall it splashes off the rocks.

There are many, many other things to see on the Neighbor Islands. It would take all your life to see every one. On Hawaii there's the volcano where you can see red hot lava coming out. Also the City of Refuge and the spot where Captain Cook was killed and Parker Ranch. On Maui you can drive to the top of Mount Haleakala, an extinct volcano, and look down in. Or you can drive along a cliff to Hana where there's a waterfall around every corner. Kauai has a Spouting Horn where the water shoots up through a hole by the ocean. There is Waimea Canyon with trails where you can hike and watch the goats climbing on the cliffs. Molokai has Halawa Valley where people camp.

LOVE MEANS FISHING WITH MY GRANDFATHER

There are many sports in Hawaii, like mud sliding. When you go mud sliding, you go up in the mountains where it rains a lot. You find a hill going down that has a lot of real wet old mud. There are two different ways to go down the mountain. One is going down on something. For instance, you get ti leaves and put it down and slide on it. Another way is to slide down on nothing. It is better to slide down on something, otherwise you might get holes in your pants. When you slide down, sometimes your okole hurts. You can slide down either fast or slow. It's scarey to go fast but it's more fun. You get real muddy. At the end of the slide there might be a pool of water. You fall into the water and you can even go swimming. On the way home you can stop to pick guava and mountain apple.

Another good sport is surfing. It makes you excited to think about it when you wake up in the morning. You eat a big breakfast and take a lunch along. Your mother will take you and your friend. When you get there it is usually sunny. The water might be a little bit cold. You catch waves and fall off your board and everything else. When you fall off into the water you can see the bottom of the ocean, all the beautiful coral, seaweed, algae. You might surf for about three hours and eat lunch in between. Then you go home, wash off your board and eat dinner.

There are all kinds of fishing in Hawaii even for girls. There was a girl who went spear fishing with her father and big brothers in the Waimea River. The water was cool. She caught a small fish while her father caught lobsters. The next time she went alone. She was scared but she speared a big fish. Her father was proud of her. She was so very happy about that because he said she was the best fisher girl.

Now I will tell you about a boy who went bottom fishing with his father on the Penny Al (that's a boat) for New Year's. They only took one rod and one lure to use. It so happened, they ran this one lure and this one rod and what do you think? They tangled with a 498-pound marlin. The father managed to fight the fish and secure it to the boat for the tow home where people were willing to get the marlin out of the water.

To other children love means having their grandfather teach them how to fish and fix the pole. The kind of bait to use is live shrimp and frozen shrimp from the mainland. You can use a spinning reel and a fiberglass pole. One day a boy was fishing by Waikiki Beach where the wall is broken. He put on the bait and threw it out. All of a sudden, a barracuda hit the line and jumped into the air. The boy wasn't ready for it. That fish really gave a good fight. It was about two feet long and about five pounds. When the fish was a few feet from the boy's father on shore, the line snapped. It was terrific to see the fish with its sharp teeth and long, silver body. When the boy and his father walked back to the car, they were still talking about the fish.

Or you can go net fishing. There was a boy who camped out with his father and his uncle. Before they went fishing they prepared the net. They put leads on one side of the net and floaters on the other side so the side that had the leads would go to the bottom of the ocean and the floaters would stay on top of the water. The boy and his father put the net into their big innertube and took it out. They set the net. When the fish and lobster swam right into the net, they would struggle and get stuck. That way the boy and his father caught twelve lobster, thirteen manini and ten rock fish.

At the beach there is a lot of things to do like swimming. Or you can try to race a sand crab. The sand crab will always win even though it runs sideways. Maybe, it's because he runs on eight legs. If you sit very still on a quiet beach, after a long time the little crabs will come out of holes in the sand. They are almost the same color as the sand. They begin to dig sand out of their holes. When the big waves

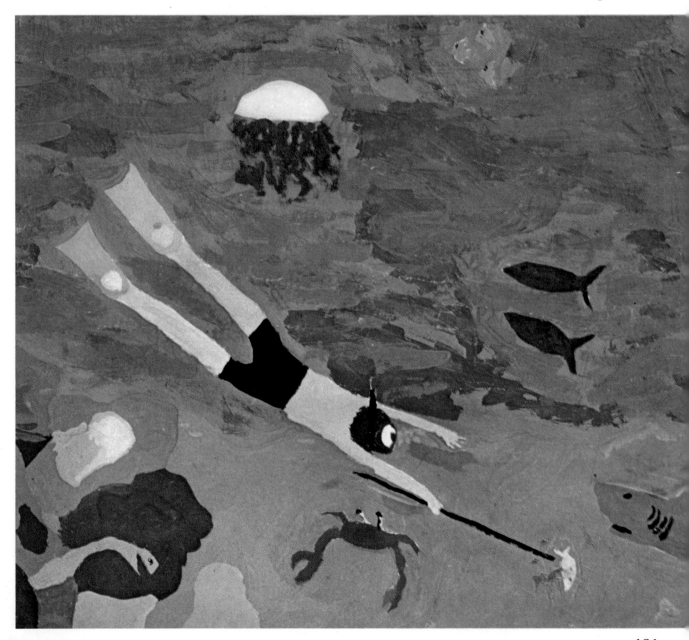

wash onto the beach, the crabs chase after the wave and eat the bits of food left on the beach.

Chicken fights are really interesting. Mostly, when the people bring their chickens, they put them in a box that is made of wood and on the sides there are lots of holes. People who bring chickens put them on the scale to see how much they weigh. If two chickens are the same weight, the owner asks the other owner if they want to fight chicken. Then they put the knife on the chicken's left leg with string and tape. They let the chickens go and they fight. The chicken that is living after the fight is the winner. There are lunch wagons at chicken fights where you can buy food.

IF YOU WERE A HAWAIIAN BOY

People from many parts of the world have donated some object, tradition or custom to make Hawaii what it is today, a place where all nationalities can live together in peace. The first people to come to Hawaii were the Hawaiians. From our Hawaiian heritage we can learn how to live on these islands without ruining them. Whenever the old Hawaiians picked something, they always replanted it.

This is a true story about a Hawaiian boy. His great grandfather was a farmer. He planted fruit trees and vegetables. He also was a fisherman and knew how to make all kinds of nets so he didn't have to buy them. The great grandmother loved to weave. She made hats and sewed Hawaiian bedspreads and blankets. Their son was a good climber. He would climb up and pick a coconut when his mother was thirsty. He would cut off the end so she could drink the coconut milk. Father would take olona bark and weave long fish nets. Then he and his son would lay the net. The next morning they would come home with colorful, red fish. The great grandmother cooked the fish and they had a good dinner. This is how the Hawaiians lived on the islands without hurting them.

Hawaiians brought many other skills and traditions. One was the hula. This is a swaying of the body, as well as hands and feet motions, to indicate the loveliness of Hawaii. Missionaries who came to the islands thought the hula was indecent because they did not understand this beautiful art. In spite of the taboo imposed by the missionaries, the art was not lost because Hawaii's people are part of this beautiful rhythm. Now men, women and children are taught the hula by instructors all over the islands.

The luau or Hawaiian feast is another part of our Hawaiian heritage. A luau is made up of food, entertainment and hospitality. Everybody brings something and works together to prepare the imu, or underground oven, where a pig is baked on red hot stones. People sit on grass or mats to eat. Everyone wears leis or garlands of flowers. There is plenty of dancing the hula and singing because everybody joins in.

In Hawaii today people of all races and nationalities use many Hawaiian words such as puka which means hole, pau which means the end, okole which means your seat, and aloha which means love. It is also a greeting and a goodbye but mostly it means love for everything. The aloha spirit is shown through hospitality. Aloha is a great heritage from the Hawaiians. Because of it we are called the Aloha State. Hawaii is the only state in the union named after love.

HEY, HAOLE!

The Polynesians won the race to the islands and the haoles took second place. As most everyone knows, at first a haole was anybody who wasn't Hawaiian. In later years, a haole has come to mean a Caucasian person. This European culture helped the history of Hawaii by discovering it and making it known. Captain Cook brought iron to the islands which made things easier for Hawaiians. Soon Hawaiian women didn't have to spend so much time making tapa because they could get cloth.

Missionaries brought many good things to Hawaii, especially schools, doctors, medicine and God. The missionaries helped the Hawaiians learn how to get along with the outside world. They brought knowledge in books and taught Hawaiians how to read.

Haoles helped the economy of the islands very much. This culture brought the whaling industry to Hawaii. Haoles opened stores where people could buy things you couldn't buy in Hawaii before. Haoles started and developed the commercial sugar cane industry here. Later, haoles opened hotels and built the tourist industry.

This culture introduced many new plants and animals to Hawaii: cows, horses, mules, cats, ducks, apples, peaches, pineapple, oranges, limes, lemons. The haole introduced tools that made farming easier and invented new tools especially adapted to Hawaiian conditions. Along with useful animals the haole also brought insects, the mongoose and many kinds of diseases for plants and animals and people.

129

The list of things we owe to our haole heritage is almost endless. In sports we have football, baseball, basketball, tennis, golf. In entertainment we have television, movies, plays, school carnivals. In government we have laws, elections, courts and policemen. In religion we have Christianity, the Ten Commandments, churches and Sunday School. In our homes we have electricity, toilets, refrigerators, stoves, telephones.

In business we have computers, adding machines, automobiles, airplanes, satellite communication. During war we have rifles, tanks, war ships and bombers. In our daily lives we have opportunity and freedom of speech.

CRACK SEED FOR 5 CENTS

After the Hawaiians and haoles, the Chinese came next to Hawaii. They brought love, pride and great determination to work hard and raise money for their families. Many worked on the plantations at first but they also went into business. For example, the grandparents of a boy in Hawaii raised eleven children. To do it they sold leis made out of crepe paper for 1-1/2¢, a gallon of pupu seeds or red pep seed for 5¢, hula skirts for 3¢, and lauhala hats for 10¢. The grandfather worked in the cannery at night.

Here is another true story. Great grandfather Lee came to Hawaii from China because it was safer. He had nine children. He worked as a laborer in the pineapple fields. After the four eldest children finished high school, they went to work to send the five youngest children to college. They also bought land. Of these children, one is a lawyer, three are teachers and one is an engineer. There are 28 grandchildren. Some are bankers, one is an architect, six are teachers and one is an engineer.

Some things the Chinese brought to Hawaii are rice, needles, silk and tea. They also brought spices and many medicines which Chinese in Hawaii still prepare themselves today. Acupuncture is a Chinese medical art.

In Hawaii the Chinese started a new language that other laborers from other countries picked up because everybody spoke a different language. So they learned the important words from different languages and combined them to talk with one another. For example, they started a sentence with some Chinese words, went on with Japanese words, then added some Hawaiian or Portuguese words. This is called pidgin English.

The Chinese also brought to Hawaii a love of good food and a good time. Chinese foods include bird's nest soup, shark fin soup, sweet and sour pork, chew fun, crisp won ton, crispy duck, char siu, roast pork. Chinese New Year is when everybody has fun. Everybody pops firecrackers to scare away the evil spirits. There is a dragon dance in Chinatown to scare away the evil spirits. Jai, a vegetable dish, is cooked on New Year's eve because you can't eat meat on New Year's. Children must hold their tea cup in two hands and say, "Happy New Year," in Chinese to married relatives. For this, the children get li see, money wrapped in strips of red paper with Chinese words saying good luck, happiness, wealth and other words. Children must not fight on New Year's Day and New Year's Eve.

MY GREAT GRANDPARENTS

My great grandparents came to the Hawaiian Islands from Japan to make a better living. My great grandfather on my grandfather's side came in the second group. He was Tsunekichi Nakatani.

He wore all Japanese clothes when he came to Hawaii in 1890. He worked in the cane fields from 5 a.m. to 5 p.m. In the fields women worked, too.

In the fields the workers wore pants, shirt, boots, and sometimes hats. At the beginning they had an interpreter. The bosses were called lunas. Some of the lunas let workers rest, while others didn't.

My great grandfather got 50¢ a day or $15.00 a month. He got free fire wood, but he had to buy his own food. He lived in a Japanese camp. Two people shared one room. The house had wooden walls and corrugated tin roofs.

My great grandfather went back to Japan in 1899. He came back to Hawaii with his wife in 1901. My great grandfather died in 1932 and my great grandmother died in 1962.

My great grandparents on my grandmother's side came to Hawaii from Japan in the third group. My great grandfather worked in the cane fields on Maui. Like my other grandfather, he also worked from 5 a.m. to 5 p.m. He didn't have any time to rest.

Four people shared one room in a Japanese camp. Their houses were made of lumber. They had their own furo or bath house.

My great grandfather didn't have a picture bride. His wife came to Hawaii in 1902. My great grandfather lived for 68 years. My great grandmother lived for 73 years. I wish I could talk to them so that I could learn more about their lives.

TAKE OFF
YOUR SLIPPERS

The early Japanese in Hawaii came to work on sugar plantations because times were hard in Japan. These people brought many new customs to Hawaii. They sat on the floor to eat, slept on futons which are quilts and on mats instead of on beds and had bath houses called furo where they would rest and visit with friends. They wore kimonos.

This culture brought new ways of cooking; flavoring with shoyu and sugar, deep frying and serving fish raw. This is called sashimi. The Japanese people brought with them rice bowls called chawans, chopsticks and the outdoor stove called hibachi.

The Japanese who came to Hawaii brought with them a love of beauty. This is shown in many ways: in the tea ceremony, in the arrangement of flowers, in the kabuki dance, in the Japanese garden, in the miniature bonsai tree. The Japanese brought a heritage of courtesy and discipline, taught in the arts of self defense such as judo, karate, and kendo.

The Japanese girls taught the Hawaiian girls how they did their hair and how to put on make up. They introduced holidays and festivals like Girl's Day and Boy's Day. On Girl's Day, families display doll collections. On Boy's Day they fly paper carp. Our Japanese heritage includes the Bon Dance so the dead people will rest in peace and New Year's when everybody pounds mochi rice for good luck. Religions that came from Japan to Hawaii are Shintoism and Buddhism.

A nice custom from Japan is taking off your slippers before you enter the house. The Japanese brought along the koto which is a harp and the samisen which is a

banjo. Japanese chess is called shogi and Japanese checkers is called go. Hanafuda is a Japanese card game.

Our Japanese heritage also contributed to the growth of Hawaii. They grew and harvested the sugar cane that built the economy. It was very hard work. First, they had to learn English. Work in the fields started at 5 a.m. and ended at 5 p.m. The pay was 50¢ a day. These people wanted their children to have a good education so they sent them to school. So today these children are legislators, big businessmen, people very important to the state. Some are rich people and merchants, some are truck farmers or salesmen.

WHAT HAWAII WILL BE LIKE

When I grow up, surfers won't have any waves to catch because the reefs will be broke. Tourists will flock to the beaches because now Hawaii is one of the places with clean water. To swim will cost five dollars and a beach plot will cost ten. But tourists will gladly pay because they are glad to see the ocean again.

Lots of things will change but we will still have Hawaii and the United States. We will have the ocean, fish, lobster, crab, shark and whales. We will still have trees, coconuts and bushes. We will have schools, police stations and stores.

145

In the year 2000 a new super highway might circle each island and we may see swinging bridges connect each island to the other. If anyone wishes to spend a weekend on a different island, he will travel on computer-controlled cars over bridges and super highways. He may also travel by ferryboat, airjets or super canoes.

By then every island will be like Honolulu is today and even now it's pretty bad. Molokai, Maui, Kauai, these islands are not really inhabited by any big cities today but think of tomorrow! In just Honolulu there will be monorails from building to building, mass transit across the reefs, towering skyscrapers on the mountains, an over population of homes on the hills. It will be awful.

When I grow up, maybe I won't have any fun. But one thing, I won't have any homework.

Acknowledgement

We would like to thank every child, every parent, every teacher, and every librarian who offered a helping hand in the making of this book.

A special note of thanks to Dr. Alex L. Pickens, Henk Kuiper, Gwen Matsui, Ron Gandee, Martin I. Rosenberg, and Edward R. Bendet

SPONSORS

Six thousand children contributed their images and their words to help make this book the disarmingly beautiful statement it is.

Six companies made it possible for us to reproduce the vision of our children in book form and we are grateful for their generous support.

ALEXANDER & BALDWIN, INC.

FOODLAND & FOOD CITY SUPERMARKETS

ISLAND FEDERAL SAVINGS AND LOAN ASSOCIATION OF HONOLULU

LOVE'S BAKERY

MEADOW GOLD DAIRIES—HAWAII

NALII FASHIONS, LTD.